Young Vic

A Young Vic Production

NACHTLAND

Written by Marius von Mayenburg
Translated by Maja Zade

Marius von Mayenburg's *Nachtland* had its UK premiere at the Young Vic on 20 February 2024. The world premiere of *Nachtland* was staged at the Schaubühne Berlin on 3 December 2022, directed by the author.

NACHTLAND

By Marius von Mayenburg
Translated by Maja Zade

CAST (in alphabetical order)

Judith	**Jenna Augen**
Fabian	**Gunnar Cauthery**
Nicola	**Dorothea Myer-Bennett**
Philipp	**John Heffernan**
Evamaria/Luise	**Jane Horrocks**
Kahl	**Angus Wright**

CREATIVE TEAM

Writer	**Marius von Mayenburg**
Translator	**Maja Zade**
Director	**Patrick Marber**
Designer	**Anna Fleischle**
Lighting Designer	**Richard Howell**
Composer and Sound Designer	**Adam Cork**
Movement and Intimacy Director	**EJ Boyle**
Casting	**Amy Ball CDG**
Jerwood Assistant Director	**Natalie Simone**

The Young Vic, Marius von Mayenburg, and Maja Zade would like to thank London's Royal Court Theatre for their kind involvement in developing this play.

This production is supported by Scott Delman and Sonia Friedman.

Young Vic

The Young Vic Theatre has been one of London's leading theatres for more than fifty years. It was founded in 1970 as a space for world-premiere productions as well as unexpected takes on classic plays that speak to our present.

Recent ground-breaking revivals include Simon Stone's *Yerma* starring Billie Piper, and Marianne Elliott and Miranda Cromwell's *Death of A Salesman* starring Wendell Pierce and Sharon D. Clarke. New critically acclaimed works first presented by the Young Vic include the multi-award-winning world premieres of Matthew Lopez's *The Inheritance* and James Graham's *Best of Enemies.*

Under the leadership of Artistic Director **Kwame Kwei-Armah** and Executive Director **Lucy Davies**, the Young Vic stands out in the city's cultural landscape for balancing daring commercial drive, artistic flair and success with genuine grassroots social impact.

For 25 years, we've put our local communities in Lambeth and Southwark at the heart of our theatre through our creative engagement program, Taking Part. Taking Part is the embodiment of the Young Vic spirit: that the arts are indispensable to a full life and that everyone should have the opportunity to participate. We work with young people, adults and schools, and engage with over 15,000 people a year, providing free tickets to all our shows and free creative and artistic opportunities to our participants.

The Young Vic Creators Program is the only scheme of its kind for multi- and anti-disciplinary artists. We offer artists and producers unique pathways to develop their craft through opportunities that range from skills-based workshops to trainee and assistant director roles and a two-year residency through the Genesis Fellow/Associate Director position. The Genesis Network provides an online community to over 2,000 artists and producers.

Artistic Director: **Kwame Kwei-Armah**
Executive Director: **Lucy Davies**

youngvic.org

PUBLIC SUPPORT

SEASON SUPPORT

WE GRATEFULLY ACKNOWLEDGE IAN BURFORD & ALEC CANNELL FOR GENEROUSLY SUPPORTING THE YOUNG VIC'S MISSION

Nachtland

Marius von Mayenburg was born in 1972 in Munich. He studied Medieval Literature in Munich and Berlin, and, from 1994 until 1998, Playwriting at the Berlin University of the Arts. In 1998 he began a collaboration with Thomas Ostermeier at Deutsches Theater in Berlin that continued, from 1999, at the Schaubühne am Lehniner Platz, Berlin. He was awarded several prizes for his first play *Fireface* (1997). Since then he has written numerous plays, including *The Ugly One*, *The Stone*, *Martyr* and *Plastic*, which have been translated into over thirty languages and performed both in Germany and abroad. Since 2009 Mayenburg directs regularly at the Schaubühne in Berlin, as well as in other cities in Germany and across the world. His productions include plays by William Shakespeare, Oscar Wilde, Stefano Massini, Maja Zade, Alan Ayckbourn, and his own work. Alongside his activities as playwright, dramaturg and director, Mayenburg has translated a number of plays, including Shakespeare's *Hamlet*, *Othello*, *Measure for Measure* and *Richard III*, all of which were staged by Thomas Ostermeier at the Schaubühne. For his own productions, he has translated Shakespeare's *Much Ado About Nothing*, *Twelfth Night* and *Romeo and Juliet*. His work as a translator also includes contemporary plays by Sarah Kane, Martin Crimp and Richard Dresser. Mayenburg lives in Berlin.

Maja Zade is a dramaturg, playwright and translator. She is head of dramaturgy at the Schaubühne Berlin. Various translations into German include work by Lars von Trier and Caryl Churchill, and translations into English (from German and Swedish) by Marius von Mayenburg, Lars Norén and Falk Richter. Her plays *status quo*, *abgrund*, *ödipus* and *reden über sex* all premiered at the Schaubühne and have been translated into Norwegian, Swedish, Czech, Latvian, Polish, French and English. She will direct her new play *spinne* at the Schaubühne in June 2024.

MARIUS VON MAYENBURG

Nachtland

translated by

Maja Zade

faber

First published in 2024
by Faber and Faber Limited
The Bindery, 51 Hatton Garden
London, EC1N 8HN

Typeset by Brighton Gray
Printed and bound in the UK by CPI Group (Ltd), Croydon CR0 4YY

Text on pp. 59–60 from *The Bormann Letters*, ed. H. R. Trevor-Roper,
translated by R. H. Stevens (Weidenfeld and Nicolson, 1954)

A CIP record for this book
is available from the British Library

ISBN 978-0-571-39038-0

2 4 6 8 10 9 7 5 3 1

Nachtland had its UK premiere at the Young Vic, London, on 20 February 2024. The cast, in alphabetical order, was as follows:

Judith Jenna Augen
Fabian Gunnar Cauthery
Nicola Dorothea Myer-Bennett
Philipp John Heffernan
Evamaria/Luise Jane Horrocks
Kahl Angus Wright

Director Patrick Marber
Designer Anna Fleischle
Lighting Designer Richard Howell
Composer and Sound Designer Adam Cork
Movement and Intimacy Director EJ Boyle
Casting Amy Ball CDG
Jerwood Assistant Director Natalie Simone

The world premiere of *Nachtland* was staged at the Schaubühne, Berlin, on 3 December 2022, directed by the author.

Characters

Nicola

Philipp

Fabian

Judith

Evamaria

Kahl
(doubling with Fabian possible)

Luise
(doubling with Evamaria possible)

NACHTLAND

Nachtland is an invented German word.
It suggests a place of eternal darkness.

Nicola My father died two weeks ago.

Philipp Our father.

Nicola What?

Philipp Our father. Not just yours. You're not an only child.

Nicola I'm not a child at all, I'm an adult.

Philipp Fine.

Nothing.

Nicola Is something wrong?

Philipp Nothing. Go on.

Nicola Why is that important now?

Philipp What?

Nicola That you're his son, is that important?

Philipp Important?

Nicola How important is that now?

Philipp Well, he's my father. Of course that's important to me.

Nicola Was. He was your father. That's over. He's no longer a father, he's dead. Don't you get it?

Philipp I do, yes, but –

Nicola What's so difficult to get?

Philipp Maybe I really don't get it yet –

Nicola Dear God –

Philipp The fact that Daddy doesn't exist any more. Or can you grasp it? That he's gone forever now? Can you really understand what happened?

Nicola Fine. Fine. You do it then.

Philipp What?

Nicola I'm not going to listen to this esoteric waffle. He's dead, Philipp, dead. And no, I haven't solved the metaphysical mystery of life and death. It's a mystery, Philipp. A mystery. A metaphysical one.

Philipp Fine.

Nicola If you can't bear the fact that I'm the centre of attention for once and you're not – terrific: you go ahead, I don't mind, I don't need to do this –

Philipp No, it's fine.

Nicola Apparently not. Apparently I'm doing something wrong –

Philipp No –

Nicola Otherwise you wouldn't feel the need to tell everyone –

Philipp You're not doing anything wrong –

Nicola Apparently I'm moving too quickly for you, I'm too pragmatic –

Philipp I didn't say that –

Nicola Apparently you'd like to spend a bit more time thinking about what happened, what on earth actually happens when a person dies. I can tell you what happens –

Philipp It's okay, Nicola, calm down.

Nicola No, I'm getting upset. Why is this idea hitting you now? Now that he's dead?

Philipp What idea?

Nicola That you're somehow also our father's child –

Philipp That's not an idea, that's a fact.

Nicola A few weeks ago that might have been helpful. But the timing was awkward, sure, it's a lot more convenient now that he's dead, you can really wallow in the fact that you're an orphan now, now that Daddy's nappies no longer need changing.

Philipp Here we go with the nappies –

Nicola Now that he no longer knows best about everything and has finally shut up, the old idiot –

Philipp Daddy is not –

Nicola Was, Philipp. Was. Daddy was an idiot. He's dead.

Fabian Nicola, we're not talking about –

Nicola We're not? Why not, Fabian, are you trying to tell me what we're talking about? Because you know all about it, Fabian?

Fabian No, but –

Nicola Shut it, Fabian, shut the fuck up, I'm telling my brother what we're talking about, we're talking about – about – where was I?

Fabian The painting.

Philipp That I wasn't there when Daddy was suffering –

Nicola Daddy was suffering?

Philipp Yes, you just said –

Nicola You're saying he suffered when he was with me?

Philipp No, I didn't –

Nicola You're such an arsehole –

Fabian He didn't say –

Nicola Shut it, Fabian.
(*To Philipp.*) Of course he was suffering, and you know whose name he was calling out?

Philipp Calling out?

Nicola When his body got rid of everything in it, like an old sack being emptied, until nothing was left, not even in his brain? Do you know who he was calling out for?

Philipp No, no idea.

Nicola Of course not because you weren't there –

Nothing.

Philipp For me?

Nicola For you?

Philipp Not for me?

Nicola He was calling out for Luise.
(*Shouts.*) Luise!
As if she held the keys to paradise. A Luise none of us knows anything about.

Philipp Luise?

Nicola You don't know her? No one knows her. But now you're standing here claiming he's your father –

Philipp Well, he is.

Nicola You're a fucking idiot.

She walks away.

Philipp Nicola?

Nothing.

Fine. I can do it. So, my father died. Two weeks ago. Our father.

Fabian And we're here in order to clear out his flat –

Philipp What do you want?

Fabian And there's this painting –

Philipp I didn't know you were now in a position to –

Nicola is suddenly back.

Nicola What did you think? Of course all this needs to be cleared out. We're not going to open a museum here, are we –

Philipp No, but –

Fabian I understand you getting emotional, after all he was your father.

Nicola For God's sake, Fabian –

Philipp No, but Nicola –

Nicola Yes, Philipp, what is it?

Philipp He's meddling.

Nicola Fabian is my husband, of course my husband is going to be present when I clear out my father's flat –

Philipp Our father's. 'We're dissolving our father's –'

Nicola Dear God, Philipp –

Philipp The way that sounds, 'clear out'. As if he was a piece of rusty metal we throw on a scrap heap. As if we don't want anything of him to remain –

Fabian If I could just get back to the painting –

Nicola Nothing is going to remain. Here, in this place, nothing is going to remain. The lease has been terminated. Next week some single student is going to move in, he'll throw his mattress into the room where Daddy died and fuck his own brains out.

Philipp You know what I mean –

Nicola No, Philipp, I don't know, down here, in this vale of tears, in this godforsaken hovel, nothing of him is going to remain, Daddy is going to be completely exterminated here – but in our hearts we're going to keep him forever, or to be precise in our brains, he's never going to die there, he'll live forever –

Philipp Fine, but –

Nicola And then he'll haunt us in our worst nightmares and make us break out in cold sweats until one day we die too, and even his great-grandchildren won't remember – speaking of which, where is your wife?

Philipp My wife?

Judith I'm here.

Nicola Very good. I thought you were already up in the attic, cherry-picking.

Philipp Are there cherries in the attic?

Nicola There's only junk in the attic.

Judith This painting was in the attic.

Nicola What painting?

Judith This painting. Wrapped in brown paper, it was behind the skis.

Nicola Fine. Once again: my father died two weeks ago –

Philipp After a brief, serious illness –

Nicola Our father. This is my brother –

Philipp My name is Philipp –

Nicola Philipp, my brother –

Philipp So, my father had been ill –

Nicola And then he died –

Philipp And we cleared out the flat.

Nicola We had to throw most of it away.

Philipp Cleared it out completely.

Nicola From the basement to the attic.

Philipp And there was this painting.

Nicola Behind some junk, some old skis. Fabian?

Fabian It's a small painting in a simple black, wooden frame. It appears to be a watercolour. Sepia and brown tones dominate the palette. You can see a square, squat-looking church with a short, pointed tower and arched windows. The sun hangs low in the sky, it might be early summer, a tall shadow falls from the left onto the unadorned facade of the church, the sky is pale, a few little clouds pass, but nothing dangerous, no thunderstorm is approaching. The street is deserted, the cobblestones are polished clean as if with a scrubbing brush, it's only when you look more closely that you can see, by the wall next to the church door, a sort of faint figure, very thin, with a hat on his head. But it might also just be a pattern on the wall, a smudge, maybe some children have drawn a chimney sweep onto the wall with some coal, you can't really make it out, the painting isn't big, about thirty by forty centimetres.

Nicola That's kitsch, throw it away.

Philipp I think it's pretty.

Fabian The frame is made from wood, with patterns carved into it. You could put a photo in it for example, and hang it on the wall.

Nicola No one wants something like that, get rid of it.

Fabian So I sit down with a pair of secateurs, because there are no tools left in the house, and bend the nails at the back.

Nicola If we're going to spend hours considering every object, cutting into everything with secateurs –

Fabian Ouch!

Nicola What is it now?

Fabian I've pulled the blade across my thumb.

Nicola Because you're a fool.

Philipp It's bleeding.

Nicola Now you can definitely throw the frame away.

Judith hands Fabian a handkerchief.

Judith Here, I haven't blown my nose yet –

Fabian Thanks. I'm an idiot.

Philipp Have you had a shot?

Fabian A shot?

Philipp With these old things, when they're rusty, you can get tinnitus and die –

Judith Tetanus –

Nicola Tetanus, not tinnitus. Are you – ?

Waves her hand in front of her face.

Philipp You definitely need to get a shot, statistically speaking people still die from it.

Nicola Stop acting all medical, the painting is not going to kill him.

Fabian Exactly. Nearly there –

Nicola You're bleeding everywhere –

Philipp Mind the painting –

Fabian It's behind glass, it's protected.

Nicola You can't get any more kitschy than this –

Philipp You go ahead and paint something Daddy would frame. You have no respect for our dead father, and none for art, either.

Nicola He'd stowed it away in the attic, your art, wrapped up like toxic waste, it's tasteless junk.

Fabian (*has finished*) There. It's out.

Philipp I'd better take this, so your husband doesn't decorate it with modern art from his bleeding thumb.

Takes the painting.

Nicola You can wrap your stamp collection in it, I'll take the frame.

Philipp Maybe Daddy himself painted it when he was young.

Nicola You obviously don't know the first thing about our father –

Philipp You don't think he could have because you have no respect –

Nicola That he daubed a cheesy idyll onto a canvas when he was young? No, that's not what his youth was like –

Philipp As if you'd been there –

Judith The two of them carried on arguing for a while, and in the meantime I studied the painting. Everything is quiet in the street, the world is empty and has a hollow core, just the thin figure by the wall, in the shade, like a prune man from a Christmas market. No one knows what he's doing there, there's no one else, as if everyone had already left or fled, as if the plague had scythed through the idyll – and suddenly I thought, maybe the dark guy with his tall hat is the gravedigger that had to put them all in the ground, and as I look at the churchyard, my eyes wander to the edge of the painting, which had been covered by the wooden frame.

Nothing.

Philipp. Look at this.

Philipp What?

Judith Here, by the edge, what it says.

Philipp I bend over the painted cardboard and lift it towards the light, since it's starting to get dark in my dead father's house, and there are some reddish-brown letters painted onto the cobbled street.
(*Reads.*) A, dot Hiller.

Judith No. It doesn't say Hiller.

Philipp Yes it does, it –

Judith That's a T. It says Hitler. With a T.

Nicola What? What does it say?

Judith A, dot Hitler. Exactly.

Nicola Give it to me.

Philipp (*to Nicola*) No.
(*To the audience.*) I turn the cardboard in the twilight, and then I see it, too: the first L looks as if it's been crossed out. A slim cross. A T: Hitler. With a T.

Fabian The Hitler.

Philipp A, dot.

Fabian Like Adolf.

Philipp Of course I know that Hitler wanted to be an artist when he was young, but a painting by him – I couldn't imagine that, Hitler as an artist, with a brush in his paint-smeared fingers, in front of his easel, that remains incomprehensible, as unimaginable as the Holocaust –

Fabian So it wasn't your father who painted it after all?

Philipp No. It was Hitler. That's what it says here.

Fabian That's insane.

Nicola Because your wife sees Hitler everywhere. Give it to me.

Judith I do what?

Nicola I didn't say anything.

Judith Yes, you did. What's that supposed to mean, I see Hitler everywhere?

Nicola looks at the painting.

Nicola Nothing. He definitely didn't paint this, he wasn't capable of that.

Philipp Because the painting is so good? I thought it was kitsch?

Nicola Everyone knows Hitler couldn't paint. Not even slick kitsch like this. That's why they didn't take him at the academy, and so he had to become a politician, unfortunately.

Philipp So the painting can't be by Hitler because it's too good, did I get that right?

Nicola The painting is rubbish, you've got that right. But it's not by Hitler. It all looks like real life. This is kitsch realism. He wouldn't have managed that, with proportions and perspectives.

Philipp So now you're an expert in Hitler art?

Nicola This has nothing to do with art.

Fabian But in that case it's a forgery. There can't have been that many A, dot Hitlers.

Nicola Sure. Someone, back in the thirties or forties, grabbed some random kitschy painting, took out his box of paints and daubed 'A, dot Hitler' onto it so he could sell it and get a good price from the Nazi population.

Judith Nazi population –

Nicola Exactly.

Judith I thought there weren't any Nazis in your family?

Philipp There weren't. That was ages ago. In the thirties, she said.

Judith When else would it have been? Nazis? You've always told me your grandparents despised him for aesthetic reasons, and that in their eyes he was a dull prole –

Philipp The painting doesn't mean anything, my grandmother was an opera singer, she worshipped Bartók and Schönberg –

Judith Or did they buy it later? By mistake, perhaps, since the frame covered the –

Nicola No idea. What is it you want?

Judith I want to know how a painting by Hitler ended up in your attic –

Nicola The painting isn't by Hitler.

Judith Then let's throw it away.

Fabian Whoa, whoa, whoa, whoa, whoa, slow down, slow down.

Judith Aren't we in agreement that –

Nicola What, in agreement how?

Judith That we don't want a painting by Hitler in our house –

Nicola It's not your house.

Philipp And it's not your painting either.

Nicola And it's not by Hitler anyway.

Judith Whatever, I don't care if the Pope himself painted it, it says Hitler, this is Nazi kitsch –

Fabian I'm not an expert, but –

Philipp First and foremost this is just a church, with the best will in the world, I can't see a swastika –

Fabian But financially speaking the Pope probably isn't as valuable as a Hitler.

Judith Financially speaking?

Fabian When we sell the painting.

Philipp But we're not selling it.

Fabian A genuine Hitler is probably worth more than a fake one.

Judith No one wants something like that.

Philipp I do.

Judith No.

Philipp Yes. I don't want to sell it.

Judith Exactly, we'll throw it away.

Philipp Judith, it was my father's.

Judith So was the plum jam in the pantry, your father picked those plums himself, and nonetheless we're going to throw it away, it's compost, it's old, some of it is older than you, it makes you sick –

Philipp But this is a painting, it's not compost.

Judith Yes it is, compost, rotten through and through. Or do you want this hanging over your kitchen table to remind you of your daddy?

Philipp If everything gets thrown away here and nothing is left –

Nicola And now I'm going to suggest that my brother and I discuss this alone.

Philipp There's nothing to discuss, especially not with you, since you don't want the painting anyway.

Nicola The fact that I don't want the painting doesn't mean that you're going to get it.

Judith Because it suddenly says A, dot Hitler?

Nicola You're not part of this discussion –

Judith You're not going to tell me to shut up.

Nicola This is not about you shutting up and it's not about your ancestors, it's about my paternal inheritance –

Judith But this so-called inheritance was painted by Hitler.

Nicola No it wasn't.

Philipp Then why are you interested in it? You said you'd take the frame. Up until two minutes ago, in your opinion, the painting was terrible, rubbish –

Judith And then Hitler came into the picture.

Philipp And that's why I alone am going to decide what happens to the painting.

Fabian Legally speaking that's not legal.

Judith You're trying to tell us what's legal?

Philipp She rejected the inheritance on grounds of kitsch.

Nicola I didn't reject anything –

Philipp You wanted to throw it away.

Fabian She didn't know it was by Hitler then.

Judith As if it being by Hitler makes it any better.

Nicola More valuable, perhaps.

Fabian The signature makes the painting more valuable.

Judith Or less.

Fabian We don't know, okay? As long as we don't know if this is a genuine Hitler you can hold your peace.

Judith I'm not going to hold my peace.

Nicola Neither am I.

Fabian I know, you're at war, but there are specialists for these kinds of things.

Nicola So, a specialist. A Hitler specialist.

Fabian Our specialist is called Dr Evamaria Günther and works as a consultant for the auction house Reussler and Schillich, located in Nuremberg.

Evamaria looks at the painting for a long time without saying anything.

Evamaria That's a nice watercolour –

Judith Nice watercolour –

Evamaria Which, pictorially speaking, matches Adolf Hitler's style.

Judith Ah, Hitler had style?

Philipp Calm down, Judith –

Evamaria An obsession with detail. You see how much love has been expended on every crack of the plaster, every unevenness in the brickwork?

Judith Love?

Evamaria Yes. That's typical of Hitler.

Judith Love is typical of Hitler?

Evamaria Of detail. Reminiscent of his hero Rudolf von Alt –

Judith How does she know all this? Are you Eva Braun?

Evamaria My name is Dr Evamaria Günther. I'm the graduate granddaughter of Dr Alfred Günther, who from 1935 onwards was responsible for collecting and cataloguing Adolf Hitler's paintings in the NSDAP archive.

Judith Nice family.

Nicola She can't help her background, just as you can't.

Judith And your Hitler expertise was passed on to you by your blood relative?

Evamaria I grew up among all these works of art. That leaves a mark on you. My father –

Judith So you sucked up all the Nazi sewage with your mother's milk –

Evamaria Father. Let's leave my mother out of this. Hitler was my father's hobby-horse.

Judith Oh, Hitler is a horse?

Evamaria By the way, your provocations are water off a duck's back.

Nicola You have to excuse my sister-in-law, she's biographically prejudiced.

Judith I'm what?

Nicola I'm just saying –

Judith What? What are you just saying?

Nicola You know. Because of your background.

Judith I'm from Berlin.

Philipp This is my wife Judith. She's called Judith, and I don't think there's any need to make a secret out of it. Judith is Jewish, I mean not just the name, she herself –

I mean her mother is Jewish, her father is a normal German, but we don't have half-Jews any more, and with the Jews everything goes via the mother anyway, I mean whether you're Jewish or not –

Judith Shut up –

Philipp No, let me, and so, since her mother is originally Jewish she's also Jewish, even if in this context that's a delicate matter –

Judith Delicate?

Philipp Because of Hitler. So she's a real – a real genuine – Jew.

Evamaria I'm glad you told me.

Judith Why are you glad?

Evamaria You can't tell from looking at her –

Judith How would you –

Evamaria But of course one does talk differently – I don't want to hurt anyone's feelings –

Judith Feelings?

Nicola Jewish feelings – is that so difficult to understand?

Judith Jewish –

Evamaria Never mind.

Philipp For my parents, at first, it was – their son with a Jewish woman –

He laughs.

Well, it was – I don't want to say 'a shock', of course it wasn't, my parents were completely delighted, but of course they'd also really been looking forward to a church wedding, and then because of 'Jewish' and church – then of course that wasn't possible, catholically not feasible –

so, not always easy, everything, but I think, especially in Germany, as a German, in my case –

Judith You never told me that about your parents –

Philipp The fact that she's a Jewish woman otherwise barely matters. Most holidays – I have to remind her, Rosh Hashanah, Pesach, Succoth, I've put it in my calendar so she can phone her people, she always calls me her goyishe rabbi.

Judith That's what you call yourself, I never said that.

Philipp My friends sometimes apologise if they serve ham, but she doesn't keep kosher –

Judith No, vegetarian. They apologise because I'm vegetarian –

Philipp No, Jewish.

Judith I find the idea of biting into a pig's carcass disgusting, as any sane human being would –

Nicola I don't have any religious concerns about –

Judith But a dead cow isn't appetising either –

Nicola Maybe I'm not a 'sane human being' –

Philipp Her preferring to eat vegetarian food has nothing to do with the fact that she's Jewish. And being a vegetarian is a lot more common in everyday life and easier to handle, for example I can eat vegetarian food, too, then we're doing it together, but to be Jewish, I mean a real Jew, without a Jewish mother? That tends to be difficult –

Judith Philipp, you're talking drivel –

Philipp So first and foremost you could say that she's a vegetarian and then kind of also Jewish, although she's a real, actual –

Judith You're going to stop now, okay?

Philipp Okay. Of course.

Fabian By the way, Hitler was a vegetarian, too –

Nicola There, you see –

Judith What? What am I supposed to see?

Philipp (*to Nicola*) That was very insensitive of you. (*To Fabian.*) And of you –

Nicola And that's enough about Judith's Jewish dietary habits, after all she's not the one who died, my father did, and we're here to deal with his painting.

Evamaria A beautiful painting, like I said, a beautiful, beautiful painting. His Viennese period. It shows St Rupert's Church in the first district.

Fabian St Rupert's Church –

Evamaria Hitler painted this motif many times, from a photograph, he sold the watercolours in situ to couples coming out of the church after they'd got married.

Fabian Great idea. Newlyweds – painting of the church – not bad, coming up with something like that, right?

Evamaria On the frame there's a small, round printed label: 'S, dot Morgenstern, Vienna, ninth district, Liechtensteinstraße four. Paintings, mirrors and photography frames, telephone number: one, five, zero, six, six.'

Fabian I didn't notice that earlier –

Evamaria That's the official company seal of master glazier Samuel Morgenstern. Hitler had an active business relationship with Morgenstern. The phone number is correct.

Fabian She knows the number by heart –

Philipp Morgenstern?

Evamaria Morning star, exactly.

Philipp Like Christian Morgenstern?

Evamaria No, Samuel.

Philipp Christian Morgenstern, the poet –

Evamaria Samuel Morgenstern.

Nicola That's a Jewish name.

Evamaria It is, isn't it?

Fabian Hitler had 'an active business relationship' with a Jew?

Evamaria Morgenstern needed Hitler's watercolours for his display window. It was easier to sell the frames with paintings in them.

Judith So the paintings served as decoration for the frames and not the other way round?

Evamaria If you like.

Judith I don't like anything about it, but –

Philipp You're trying to cheapen the painting.

Judith The painting is cheap, there's no need for me to do anything to –

Philipp On the contrary, I think the painting is beautiful. It's really, really beautiful, because contained within it is the utopian dream of a peaceful world.

Judith A world without people, yes, with a gravedigger who's buried them all –

Philipp The vision of a world where Hitler is an artist –

Judith Fantastic –

Philipp Not a dictator. A world in which the Viennese Academy of Art didn't turn Hitler down.

Fabian Yes, no one understands why that was necessary.

Evamaria 'Too few heads,' they said.

Fabian Too few – ?

Evamaria Heads, exactly. 'Examination sketch unsatisfactory,' they said.

Fabian Heads, okay, but all these details –

Evamaria Although one has to admit – his true talent was probably in the political sphere –

Judith You call that talent?

Evamaria In any case, he reached more people there –

Judith With or without heads?

Philipp I look at the painting and think – if the professor hadn't cared so much about heads back then, if he'd responded to the subtle sepia tones, to the little clouds in the pale sky, to the Viennese architecture of the first district, if he'd sensed some of Hitler's love for the cracks and unevenness of the brickwork, if he'd been able to feel it too, instead of mulishly counting heads –

Judith (*counts heads*) One.

Philipp Maybe he could have taken young Adolf by the hand, and he might finally have learned how to draw heads and maybe even whole people, he would've shaved off his ridiculous moustache and got rid of his stupid hairstyle, maybe he might even have met the pervert Egon Schiele, and instead of reducing the world to rubble he would have thrown himself into Vienna's bohemian world with Schiele, maybe he would have contracted syphilis in some brothel somewhere, or at least the Spanish flu, and like Schiele wouldn't have lived to see the year 1933.

Nicola Hitler was turned down, we know that, everyone knows that –

Philipp I think it's a nice utopian dream, Hitler as an artist instead of as a dictator, and for me that's encapsulated in this painting.

Nicola That's not a utopian dream, it's a declaration of intellectual bankruptcy, his father could have gotten the hiccups when he was banging his niece that night, and then his sperm would have missed the egg and the entire Adolf would never have been born.

Philipp Yes. That would have been good –

Evamaria By the way, Schiele's third first name was Adolf –

Nicola What I don't get –

Evamaria Yes?

Nicola Why was it a Jewish glazier?

Philipp Schiele?

Nicola Morgenstern, the glazier with the frame.

Evamaria Because in those days Vienna was crawling with Jews.

Nicola Yes, but Hitler – Hitler wouldn't work for a Jew.

Evamaria Take you for example, you might not like Turks either, but still eat a doner kebab.

Nicola Doner kebab?

Evamaria You see, you'll have to grant Hitler those exceptions, too.

Nicola But I have nothing against –

Evamaria Hitler was a frequent visitor at Morgenstern's. He had coffee and cake there on Sundays.

Fabian That's most interesting.

Judith Kitsch. Hitler, the poor bohemian artist, the anti-Semite in lederhosen, sitting on the sofa at Jew Samuel's house, munching cake –

Philipp And what if he did?

Judith Then his hatred of Jews couldn't have been that bad, could it –

Fabian Maybe Morgenstern paid him badly for his paintings, maybe he robbed him blind –

Judith And that's why Hitler became anti-Semitic?

Fabian I didn't say that –

Judith Or maybe he didn't like the cake –

Fabian It's possible –

Judith And by way of punishment he later killed six million Jews –

Fabian No, why?

Nicola But that might explain –

Judith You're casually trying to blame Samuel Morgenstern for the Holocaust –

Fabian I'm not trying to blame –

Nicola Can we talk about art without you immediately bringing the Holocaust into it?

Judith I'm not bringing anything into it. It's always been there. All this hectic fuss about a bit of paint stinks to high heaven.

She leaves.

Philipp I'm sorry about this.

Evamaria He still provokes strong emotions.

Nicola Now she's gone we can speak freely.

Evamaria Go ahead.

Nicola Hitler and this Jew, it doesn't make sense – no one is going to believe us.

Evamaria On the contrary. The Jew is proof that the painting is genuine. No forger would put a Hitler painting in this frame. The forger would be as clueless as you and inclined to tear off the Samuel Morgenstern seal. This is a genuine Hitler.

Philipp You mean –

Evamaria I know a Hitler when I see one. The ageing of the pigments, the type and the degree of yellowing of the painting's ground. The thickness of the glass in front of the painting, the direction of the brushstrokes, in Hitler's case usually from the bottom to the top right. But above all the original frame by Samuel Morgenstern. This singular combination silences any further questions.

Nicola That means it's genuine?

Evamaria Without any doubt.

Fabian A genuine Hitler.

Philipp Can we have that in writing?

Evamaria But put it back in the frame.

Fabian puts the painting back in the frame.

Nicola I still don't like the painting, nothing has changed. It doesn't speak to me. As if it was sulking, like a truculent boy covering his eyes thinking we can't see him when he does that. The painting doesn't want to be seen. It wants to be put in wrapping paper and placed in a musty attic with its face to the wall. It doesn't want to be seen because Hitler himself never saw what he painted. He copied a photograph. It's as if a blind machine had painted it. Or a corpse. The painting is silent as the grave, but I see it with different eyes now, I admit it. Adolf Hitler's dead fingers dipped the brush into the water, stirred the paint from the pot, and smeared them onto the cardboard, his sightless, dead eyes controlled his movements, he held the finished painting in his cold hands, carried it to Samuel Morgenstern's shop and placed it on the counter. After that he did lots of other things, the history books are full of them, before he, with the same fingers that painted this picture, shot himself in the bunker underneath Berlin and forever obliterated his dead gaze at the living world. The painting is dead, but in some nasty way it's connected to my life, to my grandfather Bruno, who is starving in the snow somewhere outside of Moscow and freezes to death, it's connected to Oma Grete, who pulls my father all the way to Weßling in a handcart and later returns to a bomb-gutted Munich with a limping paediatrician called Georg, who becomes my Opa Schorsch. All of that now rises out of this painting, and I feel as if I have to stare at it obsessively. It's nauseating. It's as fascinating as an open fracture, but it's not art.

Philipp More than a hundred thousand, she said.

Judith So what.

Philipp So what?

Judith You said you wanted to keep it because of the wonderful utopian dream.

Philipp I do. But a hundred thousand –

Judith That's all you need to sell yourself?

Philipp Not me. The painting. We're selling a painting.

Judith By Hitler, exactly. Your father's.

Philipp Fabian says we could always donate the money if we have problems –

Judith Donate it? To whom?

Philipp Something charitable, maybe something with children, or with cancer –

Judith I don't see it –

Philipp What?

Judith That you're going to watch your sister buy herself a house while you give away your share of the spoils –

Philipp Doesn't have to be all of it, but if it makes it easier for you –

Judith For me?

Philipp Maybe something Jewish –

Judith Am I your only problem?

Philipp That's it, we'll just give it to the Jewish community, that's never a bad thing, and then they can decide –

Judith Yes, I'm sure they'd love to build a retirement home or something with Hitler's cash –

Philipp Yes, wouldn't that be amazing? There's only one small hitch.

Judith I see a big hitch, I see a hitch big enough to pull an entire train of cattle wagons.

Philipp She said: more than a hundred thousand, but only if we can provide a convincing 'provenance'. That means we need to be able to show how we got the painting.

Judith I know what 'provenance' means.

Philipp She says if my daddy bought it at a flea market that's not enough. Then you only get a few thousand –

Judith That would be a pity –

Philipp Exactly. You need to be able to trace the painting back to its creator.

Judith To Hitler, sure. We need a family tree that goes back to the Führer.

Philipp She says the people who buy paintings like this aren't just driven by aesthetic desire. People who buy paintings like this want a story. A story that catapults them into the orbit of the Führer.

Judith Who wants to go there?

Philipp For example, if we could prove that this painting once hung over Goebbels' kitchen table –

Judith Goebbels, sure, why not bring him into this, too –

Philipp Then of course the painting would be a lot more valuable.

Judith Of course. Incredibly valuable. But you don't know where the painting came from, do you? Shame.

Philipp Yes, it's a shame, but –

Judith And what if we just take a break? We'll set up your daddy's barbecue in the garden, and then we'll tear St Rupert's Church into thin strips and use it to light the charcoals, and then you can eat sausages and I'll grill myself some squeaky halloumi and we'll all drink German beer? No?

Philipp Burning art – only Nazis do that.

Judith Then give the painting to a museum.

Philipp Museum?

Judith Yes. For research purposes.

Philipp For free?

Judith Yes, leave the corpse to science. Then they can decide what to do with it.

Philipp That really is the most ridiculous idea.

Nicola This one, for example, comes with a garage.

Fabian Yes, but –

Nicola We'd finally have some room.

Fabian Well, yes, but –

Nicola I think it would be good for us as a couple as well, we'd each have our own space –

Fabian I don't want my own space –

Nicola We could start thinking about children –

Fabian I do that already, but you don't want to –

Nicola Because we don't have any space. All those books –

Fabian They're sitting on shelves, a baby doesn't sit on a shelf –

Nicola Look, the terrace, I could put the deep fryer there so the whole house doesn't stink of –

Fabian Yes, but Nicola –

Nicola What is it, Fabian?

Fabian Nothing, it's just that –

Nicola What's wrong now, why do you always have reservations – you're so incredibly conventional –

Fabian Yes, but Nicola, the provenance –

Nicola What?

Fabian We're missing a provenance, the painting is from the attic, your father is dead –

Nicola You don't need to tell me that my father is dead –

Fabian Yes, but it's annoying –

Nicola I know.

Fabian It's annoying that we don't have a provenance –

Nicola Everyone has a provenance, you just need to look for it.

*

Fabian Round about then I realise something isn't right. At first it's just my thumb, where the secateurs cut the flesh. The cut isn't deep, a silent slash, but my thumb is throbbing uncontrollably. And what's throbbing is not the pain – that's there too of course, the pain, hot, as if my thumb could still remember the blade – no, it's not the pain throbbing – my thumb itself is throbbing. It's beating against the table top. Knock, knock, knock. Again and again. Knock, knock. I watch it from above and think: the wound in my thumb is nervous, my thumb has separated itself from me, a poison is trickling, tentacles are groping at me from the inside, I've been infiltrated –

Nicola There's only one possible explanation.

Evamaria Which is?

Nicola The painting is Oma Grete's.

Philipp Of course, Oma Grete –

He thinks.

What, how?

Nicola She was a singer at the state opera in Munich, and a party member.

Philipp But only in the way everyone was, in order to get the job at the opera –

Nicola Shortly before his death, he hadn't wanted any food for days by then, my father told me to throw away all of Oma Grete's possessions. And now I think it's because she was deeply involved.

Philipp Involved – ?

Evamaria Involved in what way?

Nicola Involved at the highest level of the party.

Fabian Is that why you wanted me to throw away the suitcase with the old letters?

Nicola Everything.

Fabian But there are still loads in the bin.

Nicola What's gone is gone.

Fabian Not really, we could have a look and see what can still be saved –

Philipp I poured the preserved fruit on top of it.

Fabian Still.

Nicola Including the plum jam.

Fabian So what? Letters. From your Oma Grete. If she was involved at the highest level of the party, that's a sensation –

Philipp Well.

Evamaria What do you mean, 'highest level of the party'?

Nicola I promised my father on his deathbed not to tell anyone.

Fabian But our house, our children –

Nicola I gave him my word of honour. I'm not saying anything.

Evamaria That's such a pity. That's such a pity for this painting. For the price. For all of us.

Nicola Fine. Apparently it was an open secret that she had an affair with someone high up in Adolf Hitler's orbit.

Philipp Oma Grete?

Evamaria Orbit – ?

Nicola My father said Markus Bormann, if I remember correctly.

Philipp Markus Bormann?

Nicola I know, it's shocking, I was floored at first, too. Bormann.

Evamaria You mean Martin?

Nicola What?

Evamaria Martin Bormann? The Führer's secretary?

Nicola Martin. Exactly. Martin Bormann.

Evamaria Can you prove it?

Nicola No. Of course not. After the war Oma Grete got rid of everything, anything that –

Evamaria Except for this painting –

Nicola But please, we don't want anyone to – we don't want to advertise it.

Judith Bormann? Have you lost your minds?

Philipp Why? Oma Grete sang at the opera, she knew them all, top to bottom –

Judith Literally, it seems –

Philipp No, of course it's all lies, my sister is making it up in order to drive up the price –

Judith I thought your family never had anything to do with the Nazis –

Philipp They didn't, but Oma Grete is dead and can't defend herself –

Judith He really existed, this Bormann. And so did Oma Grete –

Philipp They never met. My grandmother just sang in the choir. She wasn't a star, she didn't shake anyone's hand, she didn't attend any receptions –

Judith But she was a member of the party?

Philipp Everyone was back then.

Judith My grandmother wasn't –

Philipp Of course not –

Judith You never told me.

Looks at her hands.

Philipp What? What is it?

Judith The ring.

Philipp What about it?

Judith Our engagement ring. It's Oma Grete's.

Philipp Oma Grete didn't do anything.

Judith Like everyone else. Everyone just watched and did nothing. Absolutely nothing.

She takes off the ring.

Judith Of course we were never really engaged, we're a modern couple, but when I went to study in America for a year, he gave me this ring, so I'd know he was serious. The ring is simple, a red fire opal, a beautiful gem, I really like it, an old family heirloom from Oma Grete, he said. She got it from Bruno, her first husband, when he had to go to war in 1941. A goodbye ring, on the inside there's an engraving, it says 'forget-me-not'. And their initials. M for Margarete and B for Bruno.

Philipp I thought it was fitting. 'Forget-me-not', after all Judith was going to America for a year. I didn't want her to forget me.

Judith But when Opa Bruno wasn't able to come back from Russia because somewhere outside of Moscow his corpse was frozen to the ground, Oma Grete eventually decided to forget him after all, she had him declared dead and married limping Opa Schorsch.

Philipp I thought it was nicer than a newly bought ring. A family heirloom also means you want her to be part of the family, and that's what I wanted.

Judith Me too. I wanted to be part of the family, too.

Philipp And I thought it was a nice gesture of reconciliation, a Jewish woman wearing such a tragic ring because of her love for a German man.

Judith But back then I didn't know what kind of family this is –

Philipp My sister is mental, other than that we're a completely normal family.

Judith And in any case, our relationship has nothing to do with reconciliation.

Philipp Because we argue the whole time?

Judith No, because we're living now, not in the past.

Philipp But our love is a very special thing, me being German and you being Jewish.

Judith But I don't love you as a Jewish woman. And I don't love you because you're German, either.

Philipp Of course not. You love me despite the fact that I'm German.

Judith No.

Philipp And that's what makes it so special, because everyone can see at once that ours is a particularly strong kind of love –

Judith Really?

Philipp After all we, the Germans, committed the worst crime of all time against you. And nevertheless you love me, our love is stronger than –

Judith Is that right, is that official? Did you get an entry in the Guinness Book of Records for that? 'The worst crime of all time.'

Philipp I didn't mean it like that.

Judith You always want to be special, don't you? The best.

Philipp No, why?

Judith But don't worry, your record, I don't think anyone is going to challenge it any time soon.

Philipp Why these divisions, why this 'we' and 'you'?

Judith I didn't start this.

Philipp You said, 'You always want to be special.' I don't think that's especially nice.

Judith I know, I'm always the guilty one.

Philipp No, this is not about guilt. I'm not interested in guilt at all.

Judith As long as no one says you're guilty.

Philipp You're obsessed with guilt.

Judith As long as it's not you. Sometimes I think you only married me because you felt guilty –

Nicola And that's when I lost it. It shouldn't have happened, I know that, and it was against what we'd agreed on, but –

Judith What did you agree on?

Nicola That I wouldn't start talking about Palestine –

Judith Palestine?

Nicola I think it's unbearable, the way you're getting up on your high horse here, driving my brother into a corner, talking about guilt as if my brother could be reduced to being German –

Judith But he's the one who –

Nicola None of it is nice, we're perfectly aware of that, we're seeing to it, although our generation didn't actually do anything, we do everything you tell us but it's never enough, it's never good enough because, sure, it's always easier to point the finger at other people instead of putting your own house in order –

Judith What house would that be? What, in your opinion, is my house?

Nicola I've already told you: Palestine –

Judith My house is actually a flat, and it's on Kantstraße.

Philipp This is not what we're talking about right now Nicola, it really isn't –

Nicola Why not? I know, for you it's always automatically anti-Semitism, even though we're only criticising Israel, you can never distinguish between the two –

Philipp I can distinguish very easily –

Judith I can't see anyone distinguishing between the two.

Nicola Here we go.

Judith If German synagogues are being defaced as a reaction to something happening in Israel, is that criticising Israel? A synagogue is not the Israeli embassy.

Nicola I'm not defacing any synagogues –

Judith No, you wouldn't do that, and you wouldn't spit at Jews in the street because of Israel either, would you? You wouldn't go that far, and maybe you lack the courage to –

Nicola I'm talking about a serious criticism of Israel –

Judith 'A serious criticism of Israel', exactly. Why is it even called that? 'Criticism of Israel.' No other country has its own criticism. 'Criticism of Brazil', 'Criticism of Spain', 'Criticism of Russia'?

Philipp Why are you talking about Spain?

Judith 'Criticism of Australia', 'Criticism of Switzerland' –?

Nicola It's no coincidence that it's criticism of –

Judith That's right. It's the old slur that we ourselves are to blame for anti-Semitism.

Nicola No one said that –

Judith Yes, you just did –

Nicola But isn't it surprising that the Jews, of all people, are driving out and terrorising people down there, that they're erecting camps, building walls, killing innocent –

Judith Why 'of all people'? Why 'the Jews of all people'?

Nicola Because you should know better.

Judith Why? Why should 'we' know better? Because Jews were persecuted during the Third Reich?

Nicola Obviously –

Judith And you think we should have learned a lesson from that experience?

Nicola Well, we've certainly learned from it –

Judith I didn't realise the Holocaust was a sort of educational project for European Jews, to teach them to behave better in Palestine, but of course that makes sense, I'm such an idiot, I always thought the Holocaust was about killing as many Jews as possible in as short a time as possible –

Nicola That's not –

Judith But of course it was a pedagogical approach, maybe a bit radical in its execution, but well-intended, correct?

Nicola No, you're deliberately misunderstanding me.

Judith Excuse me, but how can I understand it correctly? What's correct about what you're saying?

Philipp She means that we can all learn from the mistakes of history –

Judith What mistakes did history make? Or do you think we should learn from the mistakes of the Germans?

Philipp No, we mean – I mean –

Judith So the Jews did something wrong? So they're to blame after all? What was the mistake we should have learned from? That we let ourselves get killed? Are we guilty of that?

Philipp The question of guilt again. You're obsessed with it, I told you –

Judith How are you supposed to learn something when you're dead?

Nicola Well, obviously no one killed you.

Judith Because a few Jews managed to escape to Switzerland in time, yes, you slipped up there, is that the mistake I'm supposed to learn from?

Philipp Of course not, but if we're not able to learn from history –

Judith What were we supposed to learn? What were we supposed to get taught? To turn the other cheek, to let our cities in Israel get flattened by bombs? To behave in a Christian manner? To finally get baptised and become fucking Christians? Finally, after we'd been so stubbornly resistant to it for the past two thousand years?

Philipp Judith, please don't upset yourself –

Judith If there had been something we could have learned from it, then the Holocaust would've been good for something, wouldn't it. Is that what you're trying to say? That we should really learn something from history so that the Holocaust was good for something and is no longer such a burden on your fragile conscience?

Philipp (*to Nicola*) You shouldn't have started talking about the Palestinians, Nicola –

Judith Exactly. Why don't you start talking about the Germans? Why don't you start where it all started?

Nicola What? What started with the Germans?

Judith What you call Palestine, 'my own house' that I'm supposed to put in order –

Nicola So the Germans are to blame for that, too, are they?

Judith You can't just look at the places that don't hurt –

Nicola No, sure, I'm to blame. You know, at some point there has to be an end to –

Judith What has to end?

Philipp Ow, Nicola, awkward –

Judith The Jews? Who always cause trouble and never put their house in order? That's hardly a new idea.

Nicola Nonsense, you know perfectly well that –

Judith If you think you can talk about Israel and point fingers as if it has nothing whatsoever to do with Germany, then –

Nicola Then please explain it to me. It'd be really interested to hear –

Judith What?

Nicola Palestine, the Germans, how you see it, from your perspective as a Jew –
(*To Philipp.*) Her as a Jew, how she's going to explain it –

Judith Seriously?

Philipp (*to Judith*) Well, it woud be – for us it would really be – I mean – fascinating –

Nothing.

Judith Whatever. Forget it.

Philipp No, go on – I'd be interested to –

Judith Why don't you explain it to me? As Germans. I'd love to complain about the hardship of the Palestinians myself. Or I'd love to just keep my mouth shut when everyone is talking about Israel. But then these avalanches of bullshit start rolling in and it's fucking outrageous that you're pushing me into this role with your ignorance –

Philipp I'm sorry, I was just asking –

Judith But I don't want to answer. I don't want to have to keep speaking for everyone, I can't, for every Israeli and every Jew? How would that work? For the politics of a government I didn't vote for? I'm not a mouthpiece nor an advocate, I'm not going to do your homework for you, and I can't comfort you or give you absolution or whatever it is you want from me with your vain perpetrator cult, I don't want to play that role tonight, okay? Look it up yourself, al-Husseini, Arafat, Ahmed Yassin, the Hamas charter, educate yourselves, ask your specialist.

Evamaria Excuse me?

Nicola I don't think that you can give us homework to – we were born after forty-five –

Judith When people are shouting 'Gas the Jews' at demonstrations, don't you wonder where that comes from? From what country? That idea?

Nicola It's pointless.

Judith Today's anti-Semitism against Israel wouldn't exist without Nazi Germany. It was a Germanic export hit –

Nicola If that's the way you want to see it –

Judith This is not about what I want to see, but about what you don't want to see –

Philipp Okay. We were actually talking about the ring, our engagement ring, and the engraving 'forget-me-not' and 'M' and 'B'. So my wife takes off her ring and looks at the engraving, which in fact she's very familiar with –

Judith You never told me that Grete was in the party.

Philipp What did you think?

Judith I didn't do much thinking. I had to go to America. It was a ring from you, not Oma Grete or Bruno. A souvenir, forget-me-not, I liked it. M and B.

Philipp Margarete and Bruno.

Judith That's what you told me back then.

Philipp Yes, that's what I'm telling you now, too. M for Margarete, and B for Bruno.

Nothing. Judith looks at the inside of the ring.

Judith Maybe.

Philipp No, definitely.

Judith Or M for Martin and B for Bormann.

Philipp What?

Judith Why doesn't it say BM?

Philipp Does that matter, MB or BM?

Judith If it was the ring Bruno gave Margarete, then it should say: BM.

Philipp Why? Ladies first, who knows –

Judith If I carve a heart into a tree, and I want to say 'Judith loves Philipp', then I write Judith plus Philipp, not Philipp plus Judith.

Philipp It's a ring, not a tree.

Judith MB. Martin Bormann.

Philipp But you don't sign a ring with your last name, it's not a lease –

Judith Who's it from?

Philipp Definitely not from Bormann.

Judith I think I no longer want this Nazi ring on my finger.

Philipp It's not a Nazi ring.

Judith You just made it into one.

Philipp No, you did.

Judith Don't you realise what you're doing?

Philipp What?

Judith That you're blaming me?

Philipp For what?

Judith You're blaming me.

Hands him the ring.

*

Evamaria A moderately valuable ring from the early forties. Art Deco. A red opal with a faceted cut, flanked by small diamonds.

Nicola She got it in October 1942, for the world premiere of the Richard Strauss opera *Capriccio*. A triumphant success.

Evamaria And you're sure it was Martin Bormann's?

Nicola Their affair took place during this period.

Philipp Please take note of the engraving.

Evamaria 'Forget-me-not'?

Nicola And the initials 'MB'.

Evamaria Possible. Martin Bormann. He had this romantic streak.

Philipp Oh, really?

Judith All the Nazis were romantics. Sunsets and the apocalypse, a longing for death, Richard Wagner, impotence.

Evamaria Is the ring for sale, too?

Fabian returns from the rubbish bin. He's covered in plum jam. In his right hand he holds up some pieces of paper, which are also smeared with dark jam.

Fabian Heil Hitler!

Nicola Have you lost your mind?

Fabian Heil Hitler! Everywhere! Heil Hitler!

Nicola This man is driving me crazy –

Philipp He means the letters –

Fabian Exactly, the letters! Every page! Here. This one, too.

Nicola Stop flailing about, you're covered in jam.

Fabian Unbelievable.

Philipp That's what it was like back then, they said Heil Hitler all the time, the way we say hello or goodbye.

Nicola Even if it's unpleasant, we need to face the fact that: Oma Grete was an utterly fervent National Socialist. Even if she was always a warm-hearted grandmother to us, her grandchildren, with a wonderfully rippling laughter that reminded us of her heyday as a singer.

Philipp takes the letter Fabian hands him.

Philipp (*reads*) 'And that is why I chose you, my wise and sweet one, because like me you love and place your trust in our beloved Führer, you are my heart's –' plum jam, crystal clear, plum jam – 'it is only now, in these grave times, and therefore, beloved, I love you now more than I have ever loved you before, Heil Hitler, your very own –' plum jam.

Nicola That's useless.

Fabian There are more out there, but then the neighbours started peeping over the fence, and I was standing in the bin, black stuff everywhere, this putrid smell, and then blacked out –

Philipp (*to Fabian*) Are you all right? That's a very strange grin.

Fabian is grinning and has cramps all over.

Fabian Actually, since you ask – I don't feel well, my finger is bleeding again, my whole arm aches –

Nicola In that case, why are you grinning?

Fabian I'm not grinning –

Nicola Yes. Like this.

Copies him.

Fabian My cheeks ache –

Nicola A potential buyer for the painting is about to arrive –

Fabian My blood vessels are itching from the inside –

Nicola If you're softening now –

Fabian I'm not softening, on the contrary, I've got cramps everywhere, I see planets –

Nicola Then pull yourself together –

Fabian I am, look at me, it's pulling at me –

Nicola I meant –

Fabian Can you see my thumb – ?

Nicola Yes –

Fabian I can't, can't see anything –

Nicola Why do you have to become a problem now? Why can't you just function like a normal man? We now have an opportunity, we can sell the painting, we can get the loan for the house, we can start living like human beings who achieved something in their lives, but you don't achieve anything, you're twitching and grinning as if you've lost your mind –

Fabian I – I'm really scared –

Nicola Of what? That you'll bleed to death from that ridiculous little scratch on your thumb?

Fabian Can you please call a doctor – ?

Nicola Because you've carved into your thumb?

Fabian There's a swooshing in my veins, I'm infested from the inside, the nails in the frame, secateurs –

Nicola If you're getting cold feet now because of all the Nazi fuss about the painting –

Fabian My feet aren't the problem – my hand –

Nicola You pushed it as well, if you're going to desert me now – I'd see that as a betrayal –

Fabian No, please, Nicola, it's really –

He sits down on the ground.

Nicola Get up.

Fabian No.

Nicola You're going to get up right now –

Fabian I can't –

He sinks to the ground.

Nicola You sew curtains with a sewing machine, but you collapse at the first drop of blood. Generations of men before you waded through blood for their families, for their country, and you're defeated by a pair of secateurs –

Fabian Planets –

Nicola At least stop this deranged grinning –

Fabian I need to go to the hospital –

Nicola Fine. Go to the hospital –

Fabian Can you please come with me?

Nicola If my brother handles things with the buyer by himself, and his wife, this whole thing is going to blow up in our faces.

Fabian Please –

Nicola (*shouting*) I'm not your mummy!

Fabian Sunsets swoosh past behind my eyes, the ball of fire crashes endlessly into a burning horizon, the ground is soaked in blood and pounding with a metallic chant, as if the whole earth is an iron box of sound on which thousands of boots are marching, and my thumb is beating an inscrutable rhythm to accompany it and makes the earth sing, so the dead, which are buried everywhere, awaken, but it's strange, nothing is moving, the ground just vibrates like a tightly stretched drum, but it doesn't release its dead –

Nicola I'll see you to the door –

Fabian But no, they're dead, the dead, thank God, they're dead, they can't hear anything, they won't wake up –

Nicola Get a taxi. To A&E –

Fabian They won't rise again, never –

Nicola Looking back, I made a mistake, I shouldn't have let him go by himself, I should have gone to the hospital with him. But I thought: such a tiny cut, a grown man, what could possibly happen. Wrong. Tell everyone goodbye, Fabian.

Fabian Goodbye.

She pushes him outside.

Judith Come on, Philipp, let's go.

Philipp Now? Where do you want to go?

Judith Out of this haunted house before it's too late.

Philipp But the buyer is about to arrive –

Judith Exactly, he's probably pulling up in the driveway now –

Philipp With a pile of money in the boot.

Judith You don't have to do this.

Philipp Yes I do. If I don't do it my sister will.

Judith And if I ask you not to?

Philipp What?

Judith That you leave the pile of money where it is – ?

Philipp My father's inheritance –

Judith Do it for me. You don't have to understand it –

Philipp I understand all of it, but –

Judith Just do it –

Philipp I'm doing a business deal –

Judith You're doing your business, right –

Philipp You never thought I could do this –

Judith No, I actually thought you were a nice person –

Philipp But for the first time in my life I'm doing something as an adult. My father is dead –

Judith You know – you could just chop down your family tree –

Philipp No, but it's not really a –

Judith Make a clear cut at 1945 –

Philipp Why forty-five?

Judith And just cut off everything that happened before: nothing to do with us, the perpetrators, alone on the other side of history, evil grandfathers, mean grandmothers, don't even look at them –

Philipp My grandmother wasn't mean –

Judith Just forget all of it.

Philipp No, you don't get it –

Judith Just chop off the branch you're sitting on. You won't fall, I'll catch you –

Philipp Yeah, no, I'm not sitting on a branch –

Judith You used to not care, you wanted to fall as far from the tree as possible –

Philipp I don't know, your branches and trees –

Judith But now – you're frantically tying yourself to it –

Philipp No, but listen –

Judith To your family tree, the rope nice and tight around your neck so you're dangling there, deeply entangled, and cling together, swing together –

Philipp Now be quiet –

Nothing.

Judith Okay – ?

Philipp Listen. He's about to arrive, I need to concentrate –

Judith You need to – aha?

Philipp I want to go through with this.

Judith Go through with it. Okay.

Philipp If this is getting too much for you –

Judith For me?

Philipp If you'd like to – leave –

Judith So you can 'go through' with your Black Mass in peace and panic – ?

Philipp Black Mass, nonsense, no, it's just that –

Judith I'm disturbing you.

Philipp No, of course not, but –

Judith Yes. I'm disturbing you.

Evamaria We're selling an original watercolour by the former Reich Chancellor Adolf Hitler, see the expert report, 'St Rupert's Church in the first Viennese district', around 1912, catalogue number two-six-four, from the estate of an anonymous lady, according to the family she was Martin Bormann's lover, the legendary M, dot, familiar from the letters of the Bormann couple. Relevant documents can be provided upon request.

Philipp Can they?

Evamaria You have the ring.

Nicola But the ring –

Evamaria A photograph of the engraving should be enough.

Philipp That's enough?

Evamaria People would rather believe than not believe, believe me. And you have Bormann's letters.

Philipp Do we have them?

Evamaria On January twenty-first, 1943, Martin Bormann writes to his wife Gerda: 'When I met M again last October after all those years, she attracted me immensely. And in spite of her resistance I kissed her without further ado and quite scorched her with my burning joy. I fell madly in love with her. I arranged it so that I met her again many times, and then I took her in spite of all her refusals. You know the strength of my will, against which M was, of course, unable to hold out for long. Now she is mine, and now – lucky fellow! – now I am, or rather, I feel doubly and unbelievably happily married. What do you think, beloved, of your crazy fellow?' Only three days later his wife writes back: 'I am so fond of M myself that I simply cannot be angry with you. M's fiancé was killed some time ago, and it is a thousand pities that fine girls like these should be denied children. In the case of M you will be able to alter this, but then you will have to see to it that one year M has a child, and the next year I, so that you always have a wife who is mobile. Then we'll put all the children together in the house on the lake, and live together, and the wife who is not having a child will always be able to come and stay with you in Obersalzberg or Berlin.'

Evamaria Thus the progressive Mrs Bormann. This is –

Kahl My name is irrelevant. Names are smoke and mirrors. You don't know me, I don't know you. That's it, the end.

Nicola Fine, whatever you –

Kahl I'm buying this painting, if I buy it, not for myself, of course, you understand, I'm buying it on behalf of a client who of course will remain nameless, anonymous, incognito –

Philipp Of course.

Kahl Where is – if you would excuse me –

Philipp The bathroom?

Kahl The painting, where is the painting?

Nicola Of course –

Philipp Here.

Nicola There.

Kahl Ah.

Looks at it.

Ah.

Evamaria The expert report –

Kahl (*to Evamaria*) Poppycock. I know you,

(*To Philipp.*) you don't know me –

(*To Nicola.*) I don't know you –

(*To Evamaria.*) you know me –

(*To Philipp.*) I don't know you –

(*To Nicola.*) you don't know me, smoke and mirrors, here you are, and there is Hitler, you're called Günther, the frame is called Morgenstern, that's unique, that puts a stop to all further questions, St Rupert's Church in the first district, Martin Bormann, the singer, the legendary M, the ring, forget-me-not, MB, insane, it's insane, the church is so beautiful, Frau Dr Bormann, Dr Günther, Martin, so beautiful, it lives up to your promises, you're leaving me speechless, as usual you're a pleasure, a pleasure, Frau Dr Günther, to do business with – where do I put my money, your money, one hundred forty thousand, is that too much, too little – ?

Judith You're aware that this is a forgery, aren't you?

Kahl Forgery? Why – ?

Philipp What my wife means –

Judith It's very easy to forge a painting by Hitler, he didn't have a style of his own, he just copied photographs, there are heaps of watercolours from that period, take one, sign Hitler's name on it, and that's it –

Philipp I don't know what my wife is trying to say –

Evamaria She's trying to say that there are many forgeries in circulation, but one look at the expert report compiled by me –

Judith Report, distort. It's a battle painting. Put a photo of Coventry Cathedral on your wall if you really want to have a church hanging there. A pile of ruins. That really is by Hitler. His handiwork.

Kahl Who are you? Frau Dr Günther, who is this lady?

Judith Smoke and mirrors disappearing up the chimney if you want, the painting is a fake even if it's not a forgery.

Kahl Why is this lady babbling, I thought everything was settled – ?

Judith This lady is present and says the church is fake, a fake painter, it's the forgery of a photograph by a photographer that Hitler faked, everything about the painting is fake. It's a mistake that it was painted, a mistake that it's in Morgenstern's frame, it's a mistake that a Jew sold it in his shop, a mistake that it still exists even though Europe was ravaged by a war and so many things don't exist any more, so why this ridiculous little painting? It's a mistake that objects continue to exist when people die, a mistake from the very beginning –

Kahl Good, bad, fake, a mistake, and who are you?

Judith It's wrong that there is someone who wants to buy the painting, Bormann is fake, as fake as his ring, this family is fake, you're a fake –

Kahl And you? You're genuine – ?

Lets his index finger rotate at his temple.

Evamaria She's a Jew –

Kahl (*as if there was something to understand*) Oh, right –

Nicola And it's obviously a mistake that she's here –

Kahl A Jew. I haven't seen a Jewess in years.

Judith You don't need to be a Jew to see what's going wrong here –

Nicola But you are one, and that's why you see things differently from normal people –

Judith I'm normal –

Nicola I have a radically different take on that.

Judith You're not normal, you've got Nazi shit sloshing through your brains –

Philipp Judith!

Judith Why are you shouting? I'm standing right next to you.

Philipp You need to stop this insanity.

Judith You need to stop this insanity.

Philipp It's a painting, Judith, a painting, paint on cardboard. We're selling it and then Hitler is gone, out of our lives –

Judith No, he's going to turn into money that's going to circulate in our lives like poison –

Philipp Exactly, money. An abstract number in our account –

Judith And what are you going to buy with it? A house, like your sister? Do you want to live in a house that Hitler paid for? Do you want to have a barbecue on Hitler's terrace, float in Hitler's tub and father children in Hitler's bedroom?

Evamaria You're doing that already –

Judith Me? No –

Evamaria Hitler is written into Germany's DNA, without his vision our country would be a pasture with grazing sheep. During the twelve years of his government he confiscated Jewish wealth, introduced forced labour, and conducted human experiments on concentration camp inmates in order to lay the foundation for the current economic vitality of German industry. Everything you possess, everything you're surrounded by, only exists because of Hitler.

Judith You too, you only exist because of Hitler.

Philipp Just because we're selling a painting like this doesn't mean you're a Nazi –

Judith No, you're Nazis without the painting as well. (*To Philipp.*) You're a fine specimen of a Nazi.

Philipp I'm not a specimen.

Evamaria Where would we be if we accuse everyone who admires Hitler of being a Nazi? The democratic culture of our country depends on free speech and respect, even for the opinions of those who hold different opinions to our own.

Kahl It's just a painting. A pretty painting. The name of the painter? Smoke and mirrors. I mean, we still listen to Richard Wagner's music –

Philipp (*to Judith*) Exactly –

Judith Why 'exactly'? I don't listen to Wagner –

Kahl Or Chopin? We enjoy Tchaikovsky and Schumann and even had his wife Clara on our hundred-mark note –

Nicola Schumann, why Schumann – ?

Kahl We sometimes listen to Pfitzner's *Palestrina* –

Judith Not if we can help it –

Kahl And listen in awe when Furtwängler is conducting, or Karajan, they were titans, only Thielemann comes anywhere close –

Judith Well, well –

Kahl We celebrate Luther anniversaries, believe in Luther's Bible, we've got cities called 'Luther-cities', gymnastic clubs called Jahn, streets are called Bismarck and schools Pestalozzi –

Judith I don't do gymnastics, and Luther –

Kahl We study Heidegger, Kant, Fichte, Schopenhauer, Hegel and Voltaire –

Nicola Of course, Kant, Voltaire, that's the Enlightenment –

Kahl It's just that Voltaire, who is so enlightened, thinks that 'the Jewish nation' is 'the most contemptible that the world has ever seen'.

Nicola Is that right?

Kahl Of course that's pretty strong stuff, luckily somewhere else he also says, 'Still, we ought not to burn them,' which is nice of him, although, how did he come up with this idea in the first place? Anyway, we let our minds be tickled by his sharp quill, and we pretend we've read Karl Marx or Ferdinand Lassalle, both of them Jews, but nonetheless, like nearly all socialists, Jew-haters, I guess you have to choose between Judaism and the working class, I mean we worship Goethe, too –

Nicola Goethe – ?

Kahl Who furiously fought against civil rights for Jews, and we read Chaucer's *Canterbury Tales* and *Grimms' Fairy Tales* and novels by Dostoevsky, Fontane and Charles Dickens, we read Achim von Arnim, Clemens Brentano, Gottfried Benn, T. S. Eliot, Ezra Pound, and of course Céline is a ground-breaking novelist, even more daring than Thomas Mann, who considered Jews 'a degenerate race', but his brother Heinrich is even more outrageous, he was also a great writer, we won't forget that, we'd rather forget that he was also a great hater of Jews, and Gerhart Hauptmann's plays are performed up and down the country, we do Strindberg and Oscar Wilde, in our museums we hang paintings by Emil Nolde, Edgar Degas, Pierre-Auguste Renoir, and in Berlin Albert Speer's street lights still light the streets and have landmark status –

Judith What are you trying to tell us with these names?

Kahl Despisers of Jews, enemies of Jews, haters of Jews, all of them.

Judith Seems to be your area of expertise –

Kahl You're getting up on your high horse, but you're not familiar with the classics –

Nicola Schumann – really?

Kahl You can read all about it if you want to know more, but do you –?

Philipp There's hardly anyone left –

Judith If it bothers you then you can just listen to Mendelssohn –

Kahl Don't get me wrong, I'm not blaming anyone, but if you only want to enjoy art by morally irreproachable artists – do you know what the Expressionists did with their underage models? Do you want to know? No. Stick to the work of art, the creation is more intelligent than its creator. We need to separate the two, otherwise we'll throw out all of Western civilisation –

Judith But this isn't about Western civilisation, it's about the kitsch flea-market daubings of a hobby painter and mass murderer, no great loss if we throw it out the window –

Kahl This idyllic little scene made from cardboard and dabs of paint is more intelligent than Adolf Hitler, I'm releasing it from its evil creator –

Judith What's intelligent about this painting? The way the church sits there like it's defecating right in the middle of Vienna's first district?

Kahl That's your imagination –

Judith And what's yours?

Kahl I don't need imagination, I'm not an artist, I'm a buyer, I'm innocently buying this painting, it's not anti-Semitic –

Judith No. But you're spending a lot of money because you think it was painted by an infamous anti-Semite.

Kahl A tragic figure I'm interested in, yes –

Judith What if I told you the painting wasn't actually by Hitler – ?

Kahl You've already said that –

Judith Take another look at the signature. The painting isn't by Hitler. It's by a painter called Hiller.

Kahl Hiller?

Judith A, dot Hiller. You didn't look properly. It doesn't say Hitler, it says Hiller.

Philipp Bullshit.

Judith Anton Hiller.

Philipp You yourself said –

Nicola There is no Hiller –

Judith Anton Hiller. Painter and sculptor, born 1893, I looked it up, only four years younger than Hitler. In his early twenties Anton Hiller painted St Rupert's Church in Vienna.

Kahl But I see a T, not an L. Hitler, not Hiller.

Judith An optical illusion. A smudge. Dirt.

Kahl The cross really is quite small, but Frau Dr Günther's expert report –

Evamaria Out of the question, the yellowing, the direction of the brushstrokes from the bottom –

Kahl The frame by Samuel Morgenstern –

Judith In any case. Would you buy a St Rupert's Church by Anton Hiller? For the same price? The work of art separated from the artist?

Nicola That's a T. We all saw it. It's not a smudge –

Judith Hiller is a much more important artist than Hitler. He created the Kindl fountain at Habsburgerplatz in Munich. And lots of pretty naked women in bronze, one of them is even exhibited in the Lenbachhaus in Munich –

Nicola A cross, it's obvious: T.

Judith Would you buy it if it wasn't by Hitler?

Kahl No, not at all. I want this watercolour because it's by Hitler. There's no question about it.

Judith Exactly. So much for names are smoke and mirrors –

Kahl But not because I worship Hitler as a politician, but as an artist. Is that so difficult to believe?

Judith Yes.

Kahl Because you can't separate the two.

Judith It's true, I can't. I don't know what there is I could separate. A work of art is only what an artist says, if there is no artist, there is silence –

Kahl No, there are works of art that speak to me although I don't even know who the artist is.

Judith Of course, there are also people that talk to you although you don't know them. And yet you know there's someone there who is speaking to you.

Kahl But what matters is what is being said, not who says it.

Judith 'I love you.'

Kahl Really?

Judith When I tell you that it provokes a different emotion in you than when, for example, your wife tells you –

Kahl My wife –

Judith Or, for example Frau Dr Günther –

Kahl That's true –

Judith And when my husband tells you he loves you, that's also different, the effect changes according to who is speaking, there's no statement without the person making the statement, there's no art without the artist –

Kahl But the artist died a long time ago and needn't concern us any more –

Judith But he's still talking to you, and you're dying to hear what he's saying, that's the fascinating thing about art, the communication with the dead, dead Hitler is lying to you from the afterworld, and you're actually willing to pay for it.

Kahl He's lying?

Judith Yes, of course, this painting is a brazen lie –

Kahl Why? The church looked exactly how he painted it, it probably still looks the same even today –

Judith But when someone tells you something about an idyllic brick wall standing in front of a balmy spring sky with cotton-wool clouds while his heart is full of raging bloodlust, then that's a lie, and in art lies are called kitsch –

Kahl Fine, we all know kitsch is a matter of taste, because it's not just about who says something, but also to whom it is said. And if Hitler speaks to me then of course it's an entirely different thing than when he speaks to you –

Judith Why?

Kahl I'm not a Jew. I look at this painting entirely without prejudice –

Judith Of course being free of prejudice is amazing –

Kahl I don't have a problem with anti-Semitism. On the contrary, you for example, I find you very attractive. Precisely because you're a Jew.

Judith You mean because you're a racist –

Evamaria So we all agree: this painting is an original, painted by Adolf Hitler's hand, all scruples, also of a moral nature, have been silenced, they lie, as does the assessment of the painting's artistic quality, in the realm of subjective taste, and are irrelevant to the completion of the sale and therefore not subject to negotiation.

Kahl I'm not a racist, I like black women too, and Asian women. And I find you delightful.

Judith Because I'm Jewish, the beautiful, sensuous Jewish woman, a racist cliché –

Kahl Nonetheless you are a beautiful, sensuous Jewish woman –

Judith Who doesn't want your money. Confusing, isn't it, seeing as the Jews as a race are pathologically greedy and think of nothing but money?

Kahl When this is all over, when I've wrapped the painting in an old blanket and stowed it in my car, may I take you out to dinner?

Judith Me?

Philipp Who?

Kahl I want to clear this up for good –

Philipp What?

Kahl That I'm a racist. I have a lot of money, but I still have feelings –

Judith I'm not having dinner with you, you can't always clear things up –

Kahl I might have been a bit maladroit, I've never had a Jewish woman – French women, yes, American women, too, English women and even Russian women, but a Jewish woman –

Philipp This Jewish woman is my wife –

Kahl That's all right, I like her. She's so oriental in her effervescent rage –

Judith Oriental?

Philipp This is not a bazaar, she's not for sale –

Kahl I like to solve problems with money instead of with violence.

Judith Violence – ?

Kahl Let me make you an offer –

Judith No.

Kahl (*to Philipp*) A serious, respectable offer. I'll add another fifty thousand, your wife has dinner with me and we'll clear this up.

Philipp Whether you're a racist – ?

Judith I fail to see what's respectable about this proposal –

Kahl (*to Judith*) No need to thank me. Two hundred thousand. A restaurant with stars.

Nicola Two hundred thousand?

Judith The man is trying to be funny –

Kahl No –

Evamaria We have a bid of two hundred thousand.

Kahl Two hundred thousand.

Judith What are you trying to prove?

Kahl Two hundred thousand and this sale will become civilised again –

Judith Civilised –

Nicola Of course we're going to accept your offer. Philipp?

Philipp Are we? I don't know –

Judith You don't know? What is it you don't know?

Philipp What you think of his suggestion –

Judith You don't know?

Philipp You don't really seem convinced.
(*To Kahl.*) Just so we don't misunderstand each other: we're talking about an ordinary dinner –

Kahl An extraordinarily good dinner, an excellent one –

Philipp A dinner in a normal restaurant open to the public, you pay the bill and afterwards all parties involved go home –

Kahl The only parties involved would be your wife and me, where she goes after the dinner is entirely her choice, she's a healthy, free, confident woman –

Philipp (*to Judith*) So then you just go home and that's it.

Judith You want me to have dinner with this man –

Philipp Yes, no, of course not, Judith –

Judith Are you sure that's what you want?

Philipp But Judith, we're adults, and two hundred thousand, Judith, it's two hundred thousand –

Judith I can't tell you where I'm going to go after this dinner –

Kahl I'm glad you're saying yes. I just want to ease the tension. I sense that the sale of this painting upsets you. I'm sorry about that. A conversation *à deux*, without the whole group of heirs –

Judith If you want to ease the tension you'll destroy the painting. Buy it for all I care, but then take a sponge and wash the daubing from the cardboard or throw it into the fire –

Kahl I'm buying the painting. Nothing is going to stop me from buying it. The only question is, at what price.

Judith I'll have dinner with you if you destroy the painting after.

Kahl I have no intention of doing that.

Judith Destroy it and I'll come back to your hotel after dinner.

Philipp Judith!

Judith Two hundred thousand, Philipp –

Kahl You're trying to provoke me –

Judith It's a respectable, serious proposal.

Philipp My wife is not going to come to your –

Judith Dear God, Philipp, we're adults, two hundred thousand. You can donate the money, some good cause, you like those –

Kahl But wouldn't that be a ruinous deal for me?

Judith You think? If you let me destroy it my body is yours, all night –

Kahl But that's not – I would have swathed you in conversation like a tuft of grass in a calf's tongue, I would have seduced you – with food, wine, with stars –

Judith And now I'm seducing you, I'm the beautiful Jewish woman –

Kahl But it's as if you're not interested in me, as if you're only doing it for the painting –

Judith Why else would I do it?

Kahl As if it's all about Hitler, and not about me –

Judith Does that hurt your feelings? That you're not fit to hold a candle to the Führer –

Philipp You'd be in bed with Hitler, is that what you want?

Judith And later I'd kill him.

Kahl I'm not comfortable with this, it's as if I was –

Judith It's what you actually want: to be Hitler. For one night.

Nicola I told you from the outset, the woman isn't normal.

Kahl I'm not doing this –

Nicola Perverted, mentally ill –

Evamaria Destroying the painting, vandalism –

Judith (*to Kahl*) Then leave it here. You're not going to get the painting without me. Have a look at what you're missing, aren't we pretty as a picture?

She presents the painting and herself.

Kahl (*to Philipp*) Is that how you see it as well?

Nicola Philipp, your wife needs to leave.

Philipp And then it happens. I grab my wife's arm –

Judith Ouch! You're hurting me –

Philipp And drag her –

Judith Let me go. I'm leaving now. I'm leaving. You don't have to call the Gestapo. I'm leaving, and then I'll be gone.

Philipp And lead her from the room –

Judith When Samuel Morgenstern, the Jewish glazier, was forcibly dispossessed in 1938, he wrote a letter to Hitler and begged his old business associate to save him from the camps. 'Jew', exclamation mark, some clerk wrote in the margin of the letter. People are smoke and mirrors. The sun has set on the Western world, no morning star is going to rise, it's dark now, a Nachtland –

Judith has disappeared into the bathroom. No one has noticed that she's taken the painting.

Philipp Once she's in the bathroom I turn the key. A reflex, no evil intentions.

Nicola The key is on the outside, because I wanted access in case our father slipped in the bathroom –

Philipp Our father –

Nicola This sudden silence –

Philipp Heavenly silence. All of a sudden. As if suddenly all powers had deserted her.

Kahl Is the door locked?

Nicola Don't worry.

Evamaria We have a bid of two hundred thousand.

Kahl The requirements are obviously no longer met.

Nicola I've already accepted the offer –

Kahl But it was tied to a condition –

Nicola You could have dinner with me –

Kahl Are you Jewish?

Evamaria No one ever said your escort needed to have a particular racial affiliation –

Philipp After all, you're not a racist, are you?

Kahl Of course not, a racist would hardly want to take a Jewish woman –

Nicola We know what racism is –

Evamaria It wouldn't be very nice if it made the rounds that, due to racist reasons, the agreed price for this very special painting wasn't paid in full, would it? This terrible time is behind us –

Nicola What did you say, what line of business are you in – ?

Kahl I'll pay one hundred and sixty thousand for the painting by Adolf Hitler.

Evamaria That wasn't what –

Kahl One hundred and seventy. Let's get it over with.

Evamaria Fine.

Nicola Fine.

Philipp Fine.

Kahl Fine. And we'll be professional and discreet about it.

Evamaria The selling party will receive the purchase price from the bidder, and an invoice from me for the commission of nine per cent of the hammer price, so fifteen thousand three hundred euros. The commission includes potential resale tax rights amounting to one point eight per cent. The sum is payable within a fortnight, into the account specified. Mine. Given the emotional effort, I consider this an adequate compensation. One hundred and seventy thousand euros. If only he could have lived to see this.

She leaves.

Nicola Thank you.

Kahl Now it's mine. Including the frame, which surrounds the painting in an understated yet graceful manner. The watercolour 'St Rupert's Church in the first Viennese district' fills a gap in my collection and will get an attractive spot next to a taxidermied specimen from German South-West Africa.

He leaves.

Philipp We did well.

Nicola Yes.

Philipp I want to give you something –

Nicola We've just given ourselves a present –

Philipp Here –

Offers her the ring.

Nicola What is this?

Philipp You fought like a soldier –

Nicola The ring –

Philipp Yes, you should have it now –

Nicola But it belongs to your wife –

Philipp Over –

Nicola Forget-me-not –

Philipp She should never have had it –

Nicola A mistake –

Philipp It was meant for you from the beginning –

Nicola I briefly think of my husband –

Philipp I don't think he'll mind you –

Nicola Fabian. He's in hospital with an erect arm, probably tetanus. No one knows in what state I'm going to get him back from the clinic, if at all. He would have loved to have children, although he didn't even know how to, I felt like a training device, as soon as I showed any kind of reaction he went faster, faster and faster, and then of course none of it was nice any more, I think I could easily have driven him to collapse with a few movements and sighs, I'm so terribly lonely –

Philipp Give me your hand –

Nicola Philipp –

He puts the ring on her finger. They kiss. Wagner music.

Kahl (*is back*) The painting –

Nicola What?

Kahl You never gave me the painting –

Philipp The painting –

Kahl Exactly, how could I forget?

Philipp It's not here.

Nicola You must've taken it already –

Kahl I stand before you exactly how I left: without a painting –

Nicola Because you only had eyes for the woman –

Kahl Exactly: the last time I saw it was with your wife, she held it up to the light like this – and did this – and with her hips she did this – an unforgettable sight –

Nicola And then she disappeared into the bathroom.

Philipp The bathroom –

Nicola You've locked her in –

Philipp Have I – ?

Kahl With the painting?

Nicola I don't know –
(*To Philipp.*) Do you?

Philipp I can't remember.
(*To Kahl.*) Can you?

Kahl No. Where is she now?

Nicola Still in the bathroom.

Philipp This whole time?

Kahl With the painting?

Nicola We need to free her.

Kahl Free the painting –

Nicola When I unlock the door to the bathroom, Judith is no longer there. She's gone.

Philipp Gone?

Kahl What do you mean, gone?

Nicola She's no longer in here.

Philipp But the bathroom doesn't have a window –

Nicola No. It's a windowless bathroom, with white tiles all the way round to above eye level, but nothing is really clean. There's black mould growing from some of the grout, a yellowing plastic stool sits under the shower, water is dripping onto blue floor tiles covered in curly grey hairs. There's no way to clean this, everything has to go.
(*Calls out.*) Judith?

Philipp Stop shouting. She can't have vanished into thin air –

Nicola Theoretically not, but she's not here.

Philipp Judith?

Kahl And the painting?

Philipp Where is she?

Nicola Through the ventilation –

Kahl Where is the painting?

Philipp Down the drain –

Kahl Nonsense –

Philipp Maybe –

Nicola Gone –

Philipp Maybe she was never in there – and we just imagined that she – and I didn't – with the key – maybe –

Kahl Yes – the woman – together with the picture –

Philipp Maybe she just pretended, because – maybe she's trying to make us feel guilty so we – so she – can control us – and – and in actual fact –

Kahl There –

Philipp Maybe – yes – maybe she never existed at all – my – wife – whatsit – Judith – never –

Kahl The – there –

Philipp Where?

Nicola The shower is dripping, the floor tiles are shimmering –

Kahl There, in the corner –

Nicola And leaning in the corner is Samuel Morgenstern's brightly polished, empty frame, reflecting the thin light –

Kahl The painting – there –

Nicola And next to it – yes, really – crouches the unframed painting. It's still damp, like a newborn.

Philipp Damp?

Kahl She's destroyed it –

Nicola No. You can still make out the square in Vienna's old town, but the place where the church was –

Kahl St Rupert's Church –

Nicola Under the slightly cloudy sky a huge, chubby, blue-hatched child is squatting down –

Kahl Oh my God –

Nicola Is squatting, with its trousers pulled down, over a pile of –

Philipp Shit –

Kahl She's –

Philipp She's washed away the church –

Kahl A fat, ugly –

Philipp And used a biro to scribble –

Nicola And the child is staring at us –

Kahl Out of blue biro eyes –

Philipp It's looking at us as if we're disturbing it –

Kahl It's sticking out its blue tongue –

Nicola No, it's really struggling –

Philipp It's a grimace –

Kahl It's laughing at us –

Philipp It's crying –

Nicola It's having a shit –

Philipp In Vienna's first district –

Kahl In Hitler's watercolour.

Nicola And then suddenly there is this woman standing in the room.

Luise Excuse me. My name is Luise. For the past few years I had – I suppose you'd call it – an affair with your father. We saw each other every day. At his place or at mine. And recently, due to renovation works, my flat was a dusty building site for several months. That's why I asked your father if I could temporarily store a painting that is very dear to my heart in his attic, carefully wrapped. I mean, there was no way we could have known he would come to an end so quickly. He became ill, then you were here in order to look after him, he didn't want you to – out of consideration for your mother – it was meant to remain a secret. Unfortunately, none of that matters any more. It's incredibly sad. Only the picture – the painting – a family heirloom – I'd like to collect it today.

Everyone looks at her.

I know my way upstairs.

She leaves. Everyone stares.

The End.